Writing the Land:
Youth Write the Land

Writing the Land: Youth Write the Land
Edited by Lis McLoughlin, PhD

Published by NatureCulture LLC
www.nature-culture.net   www.writingtheland.org

ISBN: 978-1-960293-12-1

Cover Artwork: *Chrysalis* by Martin Bridge
www.thebridgebrothers.com

Interior book design: Lis McLoughlin
Cover design: Lis McLoughlin and Christopher Gendron

¤

Related Volumes:
From Root to Seed: Black, Brown, and Indigenous Poets Write the Northeast (2023)
Writing the Land: Currents (2023)
Writing the Land: Channels (2023)
Writing the Land: Streamlines (2023)
LandTrust Poems by Katherine Hagopian Berry (2022)
Writing the Land: Foodways and Social Justice (2022)
Writing the Land: Windblown I (2022)
Writing the Land: Windblown II (2022)
Writing the Land: Maine (2022)
Writing the Land: Northeast (2021)
Honoring Nature (2021)
Series/related books publishers: 2022 & 2023 NatureCulture LLC
2021 Human Error Publishing
For more information: www.nature-culture.net

Writing the Land:
Youth Write the Land

Edited by Lis McLoughlin, PhD
with a foreword by Richard Louv

Published by
NatureCulture LLC
Northfield, MA

Foreword: Connection, Hope, and Wonderment

"Attention without feeling…is only a report,"

—Mary Oliver

A sense of *wonderment*. That is what children and youth often describe when they connect deeply with the natural world. But children seldom are asked to explore or describe the layers and meaning of that wonderment.

Writing the Land: Youth Write the Land, is a testament to the dedication of land trusts to not only preserve land, but to nurture children's and young people's connection to the natural world. Across the nation, ten trusts welcomed children and youths to attended poet workshops, to explore protected lands, and then to write about the experience. These poems are collaborative or written by individual children; some are illustrated with drawings or photography.

As I read these poems, I was moved by their eloquence, feeling, and urgency. Water falling "from the relieved clouds." A rushing river brings the memory of a lost father. Yearning to become a leaf, and to be remembered "as the one that loved to leap." Seeing "a frog take a dive, and all of a sudden, everything around me was alive!" Learning to see "when you take the time to look." "Tasting pine needles" and smelling "vanilla bean and lavender ... like I have NEVER smelled." These young poets express a surprising sense of mortality and recognition of the preciousness of other lives. "Dead trees falling from the sky." "Mushrooms [...] destroyed, flattened,/Humans make mistakes." "A tree would grasp the last of the light." Being humbled yet not alone. "Even under a grave there's life." Winding trails waiting for, expecting "a lost walker." And the "continuing, always continuing, heartbeat."

Compassion for the Earth flows through these poems like wind sifting through pine needles. Ours is an era in which too many children grow up indoors, missing nature's gifts, its benefits to mental and physical health, cognition and spirit. Too many children and young people are denied the chance to fall in love with the natural world.

Despair is easy, but hope abides. We see hope in the rising international movement to connect children from every background to the natural world. We see hope in the expanding number of nature-based preschools and green schoolyards, and in the many pediatricians who now prescribe time in nature and efforts across the nation to make our cities nature-rich.

We also see hope in international efforts to declare a child's connection to nature a human right, and to recognize that nature has a right to be. In August 2023, sixteen young people won a landmark lawsuit against the state of Montana for encouraging fossil fuels without adequately considering the climate crisis — thereby violating all people's constitutional rights to dignity, health and safety, and to a clean and healthful environment.

Right now, you hold hope in your hands. Hope and wonderment.

—Richard Louv
Author of Last Child in the Woods *and*
Co-founder of the Children & Nature Network
August 2023

Preface: A Shared Vision to Lift Up Youth Voices

I have the great privilege of facilitating a national kids and land community of practice within the land conservation work in the United States. All of the land trusts included in this anthology have been active participants in a year-round leadership training hosted by the Feather River Land Trust and its Learning Landscapes program, designed to support each participant to grow high quality, enduring programs that connect kids to the land. These programs vary widely, but the values and commitment my friends and colleagues hold, are deeply shared. My heartfelt appreciation for their hard work and sharing this vision and mission.

When I first encountered Writing the Land, and the work of Lis McLoughlin and local poets, I knew that I wanted to work with her. I greatly appreciate her experience and vision of poetry and land. I appreciate her seeing the value in having young poets be the voice of a national anthology. And am grateful to the work of her various poets who used their voices to lift the voices of our youth.

This anthology honors children by welcoming their feelings, thoughts, and dreams as words claimed, written and spoken. Ten chapters. Each with a land trust, a youth-based program, a protected property, a local poet, a school, a teacher, and a group of kids. Rather than a single voice, the poets worked with an entire class of kids to help them to give voice to themselves and their home-land. Hundreds of children participated during the 2022-2023 school year. From primary grades to high school, children delved in and delivered their best.

The land and the littles are generally allowed small voices that cannot be heard above the din of the industrial, informational and ever accelerating world. What would the land say if it could speak? Children are closer to the source than we who loudly lead with age and experience. They are certainly closer to the ground. Their imagination intact. Their wonder wide open. Their hearts believing in the impossible.

It was 30 years ago, after a poetry reading by Gary Snyder that I determined to shift the course of my life toward kids and land. On that evening in Truckee, California, Gary recited two poems that made a deep impression and left a trail that I follow still. From "For the Children" he admonished us to "stay together/learn the flowers/go light" From "For/ From Lew Welch" he shared a dreamed visit of his late friend who had returned from death and admonished him to " '[...] teach the children about the cycles./The life cycles. All other cycles./That's what it's all about, and it's all forgot.' "

And so this anthology is the remembered responsibility to kids and land, the stewardship of each and both. Following that poetry reading, I gave myself to the land through the children. My voice would be used to raise the voices of the mountain kids in my Sierra Nevada homeland. And I came also into the community of colleagues, friends and allies who are committed to the same place-based work throughout this nation. We do this work through local land trusts who believe in the conservation of local land, in perpetuity. That land will endure for all generations who follow us on the wheel of time. We who invite our local communities into a culture of connection and care, extend this vision of enduring relationship to children of this and future generations. Perpetuity, is simply forever. Some speak of the audacity of hope. Here we work for the audacity of eternity. The audacity of unending time, but also worthy cultural qualities to serve every child in every community we serve.

This is a nation worthy of such enduring ambition. It is the nation of Thoreau and Whitman and Muir. The nation of Gary Snyder, Wendell Berry, and Terry Tempest Williams. And most importantly as you will read, this is the nation of millions of children who are rarely, if ever, asked to share their voice and contribute their own verse. Each chapter honors a unique homeland and its youngest stewards. What do they say about this place where they live and learn? Please proceed and explore these places around the United States with our youth. You will discover in the pages that follow, a landscape alive with meaning, resilience, care, and hope. It is the world they inherit and a world they already inhabit.

—*Rob Wade*
Sierra Nevada
Upper Feather River Watershed
July 2023

WRITING THE LAND: YOUTH WRITE THE LAND
TABLE OF CONTENTS

Photo by Cate Woolner

LEMHI REGIONAL LAND TRUST

Idaho

Conserving landscapes and lifestyles in Central Idaho

-Russell Property
-Poet workshop leader: CMarie Fuhrman
-Poets are members of the class of Leslie Deschaine, Salmon Junior-
Senior High School

Lemhi Regional Land Trust

"We're as grassroots as it gets."

— Kristin Troy, Founding Executive Director

It was bold, ambitious, and more than a little bit crazy back in the early 2000s–start a local organization devoted to private lands conservation in Central Idaho. That was the vision of Lemhi Regional Land Trust founders, Joe and Fran Tonsmeire, and fellow ranchers Tom McFarland, Mike Overacker, and Don Olson. Alarmed by an increasing number of properties being subdivided and developed, even in isolated drainages such as Hayden Creek, where the Tonsmeire family had ranched and run their river outfitting business for thirty-some years, the group set to work forming the organization now known as Lemhi Regional Land Trust with the goal of providing an alternative to landowners besides selling their land piece by piece to developers.

But how? As Joe shared in an interview in the *Post Register* in 2005, "We're just a bunch of local guys squeezing this work in between whatever else we're doing because we believe in preserving the aspects of what we've got here." That was one of the Tonsmeires' gifts: bringing together the right people to get the job done.

In the summer of 2005, Joe stopped by the office of Idaho Adventures, a Salmon-based river outfitting company, then owned by Mark and Kristin Troy. He was there to chat with Kristin because, as he told her with a grin, Lemhi Regional Land Trust needed "a little help." Kristin began quizzing him about Lemhi Regional Land Trust, even though she was already busy running her outfitting business and wasn't looking for another job.

"Is there an office?"

Nope.

"Checkbook?"

Nah.

"ANY funding?"

Nada.

Then she asked Joe why he'd decided to approach her about the job. He answered simply, "Because I think you care about what we're trying to do." Unable to argue with Joe's logic, Kristin committed ten hours per week and Lemhi Regional Land Trust took up residence in the upstairs of Idaho Adventures.

Everything about Lemhi Regional Land Trust had to be started from scratch, but Joe and the board were on a mission. As Joe put in his unmistakable Alabama twang, "I just don't want to see this valley get all screwed up." It quickly became obvious that ensuring that the rural way of life, fish and wildlife habitat, and ranches of Central Idaho would stay intact was a priority for the community as well. Landowners began stopping by the office to see if a conservation easement was a possibility on their property, donations began showing up in the mail and the attendance continually grew at the annual fundraising picnic. It was humbling and awe inspiring to see how deeply people cared about the mission of Lemhi Regional Land Trust.

Not every crazy idea gets off the ground, but today, Lemhi Regional Land Trust has their own office in the heart of downtown Salmon, Idaho, a checkbook and a handful of staff members. Our service area encompasses a remote, wild corner of Idaho. Sandwiched between the Continental Divide to the east and the largest wilderness area in the lower 48 states, the Frank Church River of No Return Wilderness, to the west, our organization reflects our community of rugged, independent folks who deliberately choose to live over two hours from the nearest airport, Walmart and McDonald's. We are quite literally located in the middle of nowhere and our organization strives to protect the very best parts of our place.

Today we hold thirteen conservation easements in Lemhi and Custer Counties in Central Idaho encompassing 13,553 acres and owning another 584 acres across five properties that are open to the public. We're also working to raise the next generation of land stewards and work to provide a variety of opportunities for our local youth to get outdoors, dig in the dirt and learn about the world around them. These opportunities take many forms, including trips to the Salmon School Garden, a Lemhi Regional Land Trust ambassador property, field trips to conserved properties and classroom visits for special events such as National Agriculture Week.

After seventeen years, many things have changed about our valleys and our organization, but we are still guided by Joe and Fran's vision. Both Joe and Fran have since passed away, but their vision lives on with Lemhi Regional Land Trust, and River Discovery (www.riverdiscovery.org), a nonprofit organization dedicated to providing river adventures for cancer survivors. We're also proud to have helped them protect their family ranch, now run by their children Seth and Amy, with two conservation easements.

Russell Property

Donated to Lemhi Regional Land Trust in 2018 by long-time Salmon residents, Bob and Nancy Russell, the Russell property is located roughly five miles south of Salmon on the west side of the Main Salmon River, adjacent to the Shoup Bridge. According to Bob Russell, "Our primary purpose for keeping [this property] largely undeveloped is to provide wildlife cover and a migration corridor from undeveloped lands east of the Salmon River to Lemhi Regional Land Trust's Cole Ranch Conservation Easement north and west of the Shoup Bridge." Being located just south of Salmon means that this lot has a high development potential, but thanks to the Russells the property will remain largely unchanged and the stream banks, high quality wildlife habitat and migration corridors will stay permanently intact.

Rivers
By Cooper Fowler

River Of No Return
I feel the newborn fish nibbling
Vast waters full of plants and fish
Escalating intensity
Raging transparent water
Such a perfection

Nature's Beauty
By Baylee Halle

Where to Begin with Burning mountains
And Red glowing flames. Mountains are to
communicate with life. People who leave
false impressions in the Wilderness usually
don't have a Passion with Natures Beauty.

This Forest of Mine
By Trillan Phillips

This forest of mine
So beautiful so free for me
Take care of it you see?

The River
By Zane D.W. Moser

The water gushes by
It splashes about like a fish jumping a waterfall
The clip-clop of the water splashing off the bottom of the rafts
Clear
I see the fish gracefully swimming by
Bugs spawn
They bounce off the water as if it were a trampoline
It feels cool on my fingers in the hot summer air
When we float by a tree I pick the needles off
They smell pleasant and appealing
The river is calming

Waking
By Tarn MacFarlane

Tranquil
First light shining
Filtering
Through gaps in leaves
Illuminating
First song
Growing, strengthening
Into a bright cacophony
Life, flitting and playing
Calming, receding
Light runs across the sky
Fading
Slowing down
The last bird chirps
Slowly, passionately
The day fades away

The River
By Serenitee Petrick

The rushing river was so fast and loud

Louder than my scream

Splashing higher than that tree

It made me miss my papa

He loved everything about that loud rushing river

Especially the fish they looked so pretty in the water he said

The river was as pretty as a model

Prettier than a tree

My papa loved the river just as much as me

Spring
By Charli Sapp

Wildflower blossoms fill the air
Bees buzz all around my head
Birds sing a lovely song
I hear the river in the distance
The sun gently touches my face
Melting snow dripping off trees.

Rain
By Sophie Townley

Hear
 The rain pattering on the happy plants
See
 The rain gracefully fall to the ground and nurture life
Smell
 The rain softly seeping in to the enlightened soil
Touch
 The crystal clear water as it falls from the relieved clouds
Celebrate
 The rain.

The Trees
By Ellee Painter

The trees are all around you.

High in the sky, low by the ground.

Even at night you will hear the

Trees whistling in the wind, blowing and flowing.

Reaching to the sky but

Even the tallest tree can't touch the stars at night.

Even the strongest trees will be blown in the wind.

So even the strongest, tallest, smallest trees could be just like you and me.

I Have NEVER...
By Logan Hanson

The Mountain Bluebirds Singing A Song I Have NEVER Heard
I Pause
I Smell Vanilla Bean & Lavender Like I Have NEVER Smelled
I Look
I See Ponds Of The Prettiest Colors I Have NEVER Seen
I Touch
The Softest & Greenest Grass I Have NEVER Touched
I Was In A Magical Place I Have
N
E
V
E
R
Been
My Favorite Place

Home
By Michael

Halt for the explicit scenery
Only here do you feel safe
Morning dew dampens the surrounding scenery
Engulfed in the pure, uncontaminated forest

KENNEBUNKPORT CONSERVATION TRUST

Maine

The Kennebunkport Conservation Trust (KCT) is dedicated to preserving land for use by current and future generations, and to managing properties in a way that reflects the natural and cultural heritage of Kennebunkport, Maine.

-Emmons Preserve
-Poet workshop leader: Kara Douglas
-Poets are members of the classes of Janet Wendle, Kristin Roper, and Erin Christopher at Kennebunkport Consolidated School
-Photos by Tess Johnson; Aerial photos by Isaac Schuschat

Kennebunkport Conservation Trust

The Kennebunkport Conservation Trust (KCT) is dedicated to preserving land for use by current and future generations, and to managing properties in a way that reflects the natural and cultural heritage of Kennebunkport, Maine.

KCT has conserved over 2,800 acres of land from development. While many of those acres are protected purely for the preservation of their ecosystems, numerous properties are open to the public for exploration and recreation. Visitors can explore our various preserves, a dozen islands including Goat Island Lighthouse, the historic Clem Clark Boathouse, as well as gather at our headquarters on Emmons Preserve for community events.

The Trust envisions a day where you can walk from the farthest corner of Kennebunkport's forests right down to the beach along conserved property. We strive to create a greenbelt, piecing together parcels of land bit by bit, year by year to protect for the use of our community now and in the future.

Kennebunkport Conservation Trust's
"Trust in Education" Program

Since 2008, the Trust's program called "Trust in Education" has reached the youth in our community to give them a sense of place, love of nature, and knowledge of their surroundings and history. We provide field trips for the students of RSU21 in Kennebunkport, Kennebunk and Arundel, Maine.

In 2019, our programming touched every elementary school in the district, along with a Gulf of Maine Field Studies course in Kennebunk High School and at the University of New England. We work alongside teachers, principals, and superintendents to create programs that provide hands-on, nature-based education while meeting NGSS and other national standards. These half-day and full-day field trips get kids outside on Trust properties and thinking critically about the environments they see today compared to how they once were. While we have an environmental science focus, we love connecting science to history, reading, math, and English skills.

Each year, students from RSU21 adopt a different property at KCT. With visits throughout the school year, students connect with their local landscape while exploring the NGSS curriculum through hands-on, nature-based education. This program also introduces students to numerous community members, business owners, and other groups who come to volunteer each trip.

Trust in Education works alongside The Climate Initiative, founded by KCT's Director of Programs and Outreach Leia Lowery, to bring relevant climate education to students. Through this program, students take on local climate issues and engage with community members to create visible change.

Emmons Preserve
57 Gravelly Brook Rd., Kennebunkport Maine

Located in the heart of Kennebunkport, the Emmons Preserve has become a vital part of our community. The site features the homestead of Steve and Natalie Emmons, which was generously donated to the Trust. Steve's dream was to have the property serve as a place for children to connect with nature. Over the years, KCT has built a beautiful headquarters building, established trails, and created a place for the people of Kennebunkport to gather. Our headquarters is used for outings for KCT's Trust in Our Children and Discovery Days programs. It also hosts local nonprofit events, family gatherings, private functions, and more. You are encouraged to visit and explore—take a hike, go for a snowshoe, follow the Batson River, walk the labyrinth, discover the Learning Trail, or have a picnic on our deck.

Chickadee Singing
by Fiona Ingwersen

Blue sky
racing clouds
swaying trees
bobbing in the wind
chickadee
cardinal
crow
united as one singing winter to sleep
winter pushing against the sun
relentless
the sun, fighting back
making cattails sprout
and trees bud
the world is coming alive in the palm of the sun
and we are just the watchers.

A Heartbeat
by Francis Fairbanks

Chirping birds,swaying trees,flowing rivers.
Dirt paths,wet leaves,jagged gravestones.wood.branches.
A heartbeat.

Like a stone breaking down by the water.
Smaller and smaller.
Smoother and smoother.
A heartbeat.

Even under a grave there's life.
Living under the ground we walk on.
A life.
A Heartbeat.

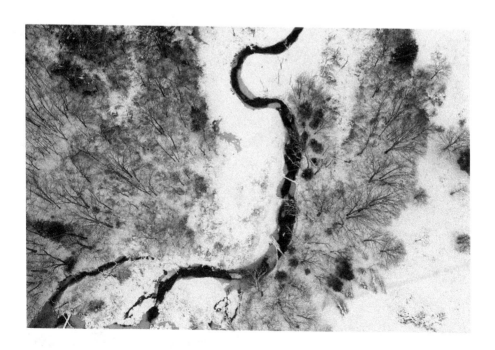

The Spring Poem
by Malek Eid, Frida Valerdi, and Dominic

Birds chirping, wet grass, rough trees

Cold flowing water, A shining light

Mushy mud

The smooth flowing wind, moving the rough trees

Dead trees falling from the sky and laying on the ground

Sharp rocks shining in the light, sticky sap dripping from the trees

A smooth hand pushing the sun ready for spring

Kids exploring, teachers showing, marching through march, ready for
April.

Untitled
by Cornelia B.

The birds chirp loudly, as the turtles dive into the water
as if nothing was ever there.
The wind blows around me
as if it was on the highest mountain, but I am on a rock in the middle of
the field.
I lay my eyes on a broken bridge that was unnerving,
but everyone made it across.
We observed beaver tracks in the wet, squishy mud.
The beavers could not be seen.
The fresh air calms me down for the days ahead.
Rocks are a good seat for me,
as I sit on the hard grass, with the trees waving in the wind,
as if their friends are right beside them.

As the Sun Set Away
by Harlan Wendle

Frankie and Sebastian, hair waving, stepping into the beautiful pond.

The ducks scream an alarm as they see them.

The mud splashes and the bushes get wet.

Needles fly into the woodish mud.

The fish jump, the beavers swim, and the turtles move an inch.

The birds fly as the sun slowly sets.

The river is blinded as the world sets.

The birds nest, the turtles hide, even the beavers swim away.

The world is dark, the day is gone, but tomorrow still awaits.

Shifting Shadows
by Stella Raymond, Lowy Fairfield, and Elodie Michaud

The shadows shift and the grass sways,
Our boredom releases as the birds chirp,
The faint whispering fades to the background,
It's almost like you're daydreaming,
Like your imagination has won the war,
The skies turned to a hypnotist,
As your stress falls away you feel like you have come back to life.
And the stress acts like clockwork,
Faster and faster,
Closer and closer.
To the end.

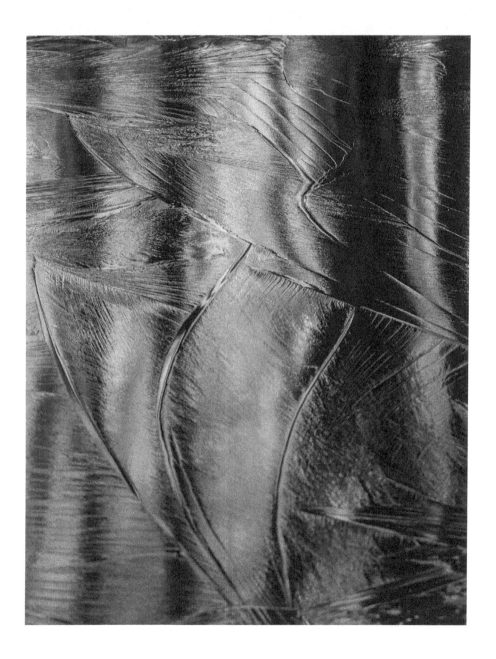

Kennebunkport Conservation Trust

by Matilda

Squishy mud flying through the air hits the scruffy bark of an apple tree
and falls into the itchy grass, not yet green.
I look over and see a gray rock chimney
I look straight and spot the trail we just hiked
I shudder remembering a high up bridge
all the kids jumping way up high, the fear of falling.
I take a deep breath and smell fresh air
I look at the rock I am sitting on and feel some moss close by
It is dried up from winter. It feels rough.
I pick up a stick and snap it in two
I realize it is rotted through,
still damp from all the snow and rain on Sunday.
Then I hear it's time to go.
I get on the bus and hear "wheels on the bus" on the bus ride back to
school.
 Now I sit and write this poem and I ask myself what next shall I do.

Our Nature Walk
by Kade Schlauder

Walking through the woods,
I'm near a river.
I see trees and broken twigs.
My friend was with me.
I saw a beaver dam.
There was grass with a little bit of snow.
Giggling kids walking on the trail.

LITTLE TRAVERSE CONSERVANCY

Michigan

Mission: To protect the natural diversity and beauty of northern Michigan by preserving significant land and scenic areas, and fostering appreciation and understanding of the environment.

-Agnes S. Andreae Nature Preserve
-Poet workshop leader: Shanley Smith
-Poets are students of Kathryn Millar, 6th grade, Alanson Middle School
-Photos by Sarah Mayhew

The Agnes S. Andreae Nature Preserve

The Agnes S. Andreae Nature Preserve and Andreae Cabin are named after Agnes S. Andreae, who donated the cabin and 27 acres of land to the Little Traverse Conservancy in 1983 so that the peaceful wilderness experience that it offers could be protected for future generations.

Today, the preserve's size has grown to 181 acres, and it lies adjacent to the 400-acre Boyd B. Banwell Nature Preserve. Combined the preserves offer nearly 5 miles of hiking. Set along the lower Pigeon River (a blue-ribbon trout stream), this preserve includes pine forests on steep bluffs above the river.

Out
by Maximus Capozzoli

When I go out
I smell
the scent of the pine.

When I go out
I see
the water dancing
in the river.

When I go out
I see
the snow falling
on the cold hard ground.

When I go out
I see
tall sturdy trees
blowing in the wind.

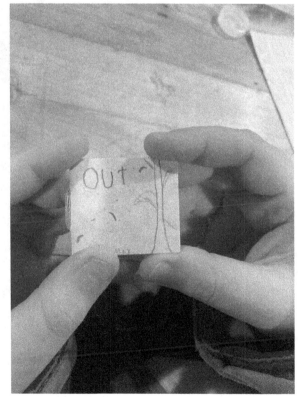

When I go out
I see
the trees, kids,
The leaves falling
And playing
With their
best friend
the snow.

Out
what
a magical
place.
Where dreams
come true.

Amazing View
by Havana Previch

We hiked up the river
We went past a gate
Passed a lot of trees
There was the Amazing View
That was the
Amazing View

The Walk Through the Woods
by Kameron Furlong

Burnt lumber
I like the Lord
At first I thought the bridge
was going to break and then I knew it was ok.

The Amazing Hillside
by Katelyn T.

While I was on a walk I saw
the beautiful water stream with white snow around it
I saw the snowy trees all around
I walked along the long stairs
I heard the birds chirping
I saw some tiny animal tracks
I tried some pine needles that tasted okay

Lumber
by Liam McGarey

While the
pine trees
rest. The snow
build up heavily
the wind blows
loud and snow
falls.

The Trickling River
by Liam McGarey

As the river flows
the calmness
goes on and
stress goes just
relax and listen
and it will do
the rest.

The river
goes on the
trickling keeps
peace while
the birds
chirp. It relaxes
your brain
stress goes
you'll feel
refreshed
after.

Just relax let
the sound fill
your brain
let the wind the
crackle off wood
and the sound
of the river
fills the air
chirping relaxes
and you'll feel
good.

Stickman
by Bryce

COASTAL MOUNTAINS LAND TRUST

Midcoast
Maine

Coastal Mountains Land Trust permanently conserves land to benefit the natural and human communities of the western Penobscot Bay region.

-Poet workshop leader: Lisa Hibl
-Poets and Preserves pairings for individual poems:
  Ducktrap River Preserve: Soleil Jacques, Ezra Oldham, Lucy Trumbauer
  Ragged Mountain Preserve: Joey Scordino
  Beech Hill Preserve: Isabel Fitch
-Poets are students at Camden-Rockport Middle School in the classes of Hilary Flagg (Language Arts), Kristen Andersen (Art), and John Dietter (Life Science)

Coastal Mountains Land Trust

Coastal Mountains Land Trust is a community-based non-profit land conservation organization based in Camden, Maine focused on protecting open space, caring for land and trails, and connecting people with nature through meaningful outdoor experiences. The organization's mission is to permanently conserve land to benefit the natural and human communities of the western Penobscot Bay region.

Since 1986, the Land Trust has conserved over 13,000 acres of land in 15 towns between Rockport and Prospect, has built and maintains over 50 miles of trail, and welcomes thousands of visitors to its properties each year through community programming.

Most recently, the organization has launched Learning Landscapes, a program that secures land within walking distance of schools, creates outdoor classrooms, and supports teachers in providing outdoor education throughout the school year.

The vision of the organization is to maintain the sense of place and natural character of our midcoast communities and to make nature, land stewardship and conservation relevant and accessible to all.

Learning Landscapes with Camden Rockport Middle School

Coastal Mountains Land Trust partners with Camden-Rockport Middle School through our Learning Landscapes program. Each fall, our staff and volunteers take the entire seventh grade to approximately eight preserves, as part of their Symbiosis unit: "Learning How to See."

"Learning How to See" is innovative, project-based learning created and implemented collaboratively by Camden-Rockport Middle School's art, science, and language arts teachers. Students hone their observation skills and discover interactions between organisms within multiple ecosystems. Each student selects one symbiotic relationship to research more deeply and expresses their learning through poetry, scientific writing and multimedia artwork. We hope you enjoy this small sample of the students' creations!

This dynamic, multidisciplinary unit was created and implemented by Camden-Rockport's progressive teachers: Hilary Flagg (Language Arts), Kristen Andersen (Art) and John Dietter (Life Science).

Learning How to See
by Soleil Jacques

What you really notice
When you take the time to look.

Forest giants reaching out,
Their foliage almost touching the faraway stars,
A bright reflection shimmering on the lake.

Morning fog smothers everything it touches in a soft blanket.
Bending the light,
And swaying the trees,
Muffling the lively sounds of the forest.
When you stand in the fog,
You can forget to think,
And you feel like you could just float away.

Minuscule flowers like specks of gold,
Vibrant green leaves like the smooth blade of a knife,
Coming up out of the dull foliage from last fall,
Stretching up towards the sun.

If you change the way you look,
You can change the way you see the world.

Artwork by Soleil Jacques

Autumn Changes
by Joey Scordino

Shimmering sun rays,
Water gurgling, splashing,
Crisp cool air in fall,

Slender twining stems,
Entwine around, trust their host,
Supply energy,

Abundant amber,
Preparation is coming,
Trees molting their leaves

Lush green, tapered leaves,
Grow so tall, but start out small
Strong capable stems

Whirling, tumbling,
Leaves descend to forest floor,
Peacefully, no sound

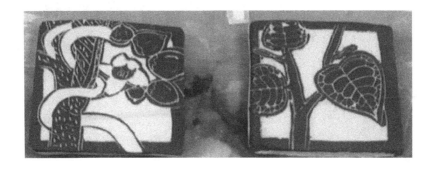

Artwork by Joey Scordino

A Sea of Quiet Yellow
by Isabel Fitch

Soft, vibrant, yellow petals

Dark, golden ridges

Engraved

In each slender sliver.

A bee

Sheltered by a large bold sunflower.

Settling in it

Like a nest,

On top of its head in

A sea of quiet yellow,

A black dot.

Slurping nectar while

covered in pollen.

Like a kangaroo

Hopping from flower

To flower.

The head of the sunflower

Turning

with the Sun.

Artwork by Isabel Fitch

Beech Hill
by Lucy Trumbauer

The windswept hill lit up,
From the darkness of the night to the light of day,
From so far away you could see that cabin on its peak
Like a top hat made of very old heavy stone,
It was plopped on the peak like a normal home,

There were a few pine trees slightly down the hill,
Grabbing at the sunrise's first rays,
It looked like the mountaintop blueberries with their hues of hot pink
and scarlet red,
Rising up to in a way as though to say 'hello',
With clouds painted in colors from pink to gray and blue,
Looking down upon the valley,
And down at the trees that flowed across the vast horizon,
Like the lakes that dotted valleys in flakes,
With orange and green leaves around their banks,

Up at the peak there are huddles of yellow grass,
Slightly down from the house with its living roof,
That looked like the top where the house sat upon,
Covered with hardy mountain grasses,
With colors of happy green and sad tan that looked like sand,
The soil underneath was dusty brown covering the rocky ground,
The same color as the tree to the north,

The tree had gentle green leaves that were kind of soft,
It had bark like a rock that was bold gray and smooth as glass,
Even though it was almost late fall it still had many leaves like it was a
forever spring,
Unlike the several old leaves on the ground that shriveled up on the way
down,
Brown as mud and dotted with the same foliage as the trees in the valley,
Some leaves on the ground had rotted away,
To go and join the gentle fray,

It was already almost the end of the day,
When the sun started to set,
It walked away into the morning of the west,
As though it was saying 'it's time to rest',
The tree would grasp the last of the light ,
Before the sun would be gone for the night...

Artwork by Lucy Trumbauer

Ducktrap Preserve
by Ezra Oldham

Warm, sunny fall day,
Stream gurgling happily,
Clouds part for the sun.

Grasshopper resting,
Triumphant, upon a leaf,
Listens to the birds.

Mushrooms, horrified,
One of them destroyed, flattened,
Humans make mistakes.

Moss, like little shrubs,
Now growing on a tree root,
Content with its life.

Winding trails waiting,
Expecting a lost walker,
To lead them astray.

The open blue sky,
Like a widening gateway,
Beckoning to all.

Smoke From a Dying Fire
a composite poem by the students of CRMS 7th Grade Language Arts,
Section 5, arranged by Lisa Hibl

small modest leaf

the sun peeks its head
leaves shatter

embers sparkling in the Autumn dew

I walk along the path of tangled trees
the footprint on the ground: size eight

stubby mushrooms sit below
lichen creeps up and up

a dark, charred nightmare
steals from the virtuous dream

I knew it was a dream in the night:
the loneliness of the tree
standing in a vast field of flowers

but clear water was flowing over silky rocks
and a fuzzy moss snuggled the tree
in cozy comfort

the sunlight was a distinct breeze
whispering
hello

the mushroom danced in the palm of my hand

Symbiosis
a composite poem by the students of CRMS 7th Grade Language Arts,
Section 4, arranged by Lisa Hibl

Two trees in competition:
the bark gives a blistering smile.

Japanese knotweed calm in the night.

Papery bark peels off
like old paint on a weathered barn wall.

Leaves surround me
like I'm falling into an orange ocean
almost safe in my own thoughts.

The fish are running, gasping for air
while the infection starts spreading.
The flakiness of the fungi is like a croissant.

WHEN THE RAIN COMES DOWN AND DAMPENS MY SHIRT
to find out what kind of symbiosis this is,
I really do want.

Tumbling off the trees,
weaving around the branches
like cheetahs chasing after prey,

bees like little mailmen deliver pollen
swaying and sweating.

Next to the path trees,
trees,
and more trees.

There I Saw a Tree, Tangled in a Woven Blanket of Vines
a composite poem by the students of CRMS 7th Grade Language Arts,
Section 3, arranged by Lisa Hibl

silver with age
trying to survive
like a fly in a flytrap

grass slowly swaying in the wind
morning fog smothers everything

I'm scared of bees I know I should be

the tree didn't mind, he didn't care
he swayed in the frosty-wind air
he was glad it was not a bear
he had history with them

Honey bee Honey bee stripes like pipes

slender twining stems
hanging on by a few gnarled roots
stripes of cinnamon, hickory, and tortilla brown
their foliage almost touches the faraway stars

the cool breeze swishes
the dying flowers never had any chances

zooming from lily pad to lily pad
it climbs back into its shell and lies down on the sea hay

cautiously examines each individual fluorescent flower

the only sound the rush of the river
scraping along rocks and the songbirds singing
their wonderful hymns to

someone as importantly insignificant as you or I

Parasite Paradise
a composite poem by the students of CRMS 7th Grade Language Arts,
Section 2, arranged by Lisa Hibl

I remember gravel crunching under my pounding feet
dewy grass twinkling like stars from a deep night sky,
the air damp and misty

I remember the mushroom sucking out the energy from a tree like a
blood drive

I remember the stream gurgling happily
the wind blowing through one ear and out the other.

The birds called, like chinking chimes.

The air was crisp, like a fresh bite into a cold apple.

You would never know the dodders are stealing the life from a fellow
plant.
          Lives? Dies? Who knows?
They are a component of nature.

And best of all, these plants give us oxygen.

I remember
I saw a frog take a dive,
and all of a sudden everything around me was alive!

Soon, the sun will be gone for the night . . .

Isabel Fitch

Soleil Jacques

Ezra Oldham

Joey Scordino

Lucy Trumbauer

Featured
Poets

Photo by Hilary Flagg

COLUMBIA LAND CONSERVANCY

New York

The Columbia Land Conservancy brings people together to conserve, appreciate, and enjoy land. For nearly 40 years, CLC has collaborated with individuals, communities, and partners to ensure Columbia County is a beautiful, livable, resilient place. For additional information, call 518.392.5252 or visit clctrust.org

-Greenport Conservation Area, Greenport, NY
-Poet workshop leader: Margaret R. Sáraco
-Poets are associated with programs from the Hudson Department of Youth: Jenifer Rosete (park contact); with NaQuera Roche and Trinity Jones (youth department staff)

Columbia Land Conservancy

Engaging with nature

When you ask someone why they hold the values they do, their answer often involves a meaningful experience as a child or young adult. The act of watching the birds, splashing in a creek, or catching a fish leaves an impression that makes an impact. These impacts are individual—people who spend time in nature are generally healthier and happier—and collective—people who have positive experiences in nature are more likely to volunteer and vote with the environment in mind. However, providing these sorts of experiences, especially for children, is becoming increasingly more difficult.

CLC and our partners are committed to providing free and low-cost educational programs that provide opportunities for people to fall in love with the world around them, and to maintaining the Public Conservation Areas for recreation, reflection, and restoration.

Hudson Youth Department, Hudson, NY

At the Hudson Department of Youth, we serve a wide range of our community's youth starting from age 5 and leading to adulthood. Through our programming, we help our participants develop better social skills, become leaders, gain greater knowledge of themselves, and foster lifelong relationships. Families looking to find meaningful, culturally-informed, and potentially transformative youth programs will find that at the Department of Youth. The department offers various opportunities to engage in programming, from our afterschool programs to Oakdale Summer Camp, our Bike Coop, and our many different community events and trips. Activities include art, circus, dancing and movement, singing, audio/visual skills, athletics, and more. Our programming aims to point young people towards activities that are not only fun but also offer opportunities to develop skills, passions, and abilities that will last a lifetime.

Greenport Conservation Area, 319 Joslen Blvd, Greenport, NY

Greenport Conservation Area is located in beautiful Columbia County, which is nestled between the Catskills and Berkshires along the Hudson River north of New York City. This over-700 acre site includes eight miles of trails and features beautiful Hudson River and Catskill Mountain views, forests, and open meadows. The remains of a once-active brickyard can be seen along the Brickyard Trail. There are two gazebos, several benches, and a picnic area located along the Access for All Trail.

Evidence of past land use is all over the site, including agriculture since the late 1600s and clay mining and brick-making at the turn of the twentieth century.

A Collage of Thoughts and Words from Children that Entered Greenport Forest in Fall

A Found Poem

Lovingly compiled by Margaret R. Sáraco

Poetic Contributors: Jah'Leigha McSween, Alyce Kelly,
and Quran Blocker

Part I: The Walk In

Today tastes like a strawberry
with my red shoes on.
Someone is eating something that is growing,
somewhere

(I'm hungry)

Wait! I see a grasshopper
A grass hopper
We see grasshoppers with binoculars.

The long walk in

(some of us have shorter legs)

to the wooden gazebo
overlooking the Hudson

Part II: There

George the dog is here
Is he a terrier?
Running in circles. He's not a fluffy dog
No foo, foo for George.
Does he think we are all dogs
We run and play.

I hear a grasshopper, crickets, birds,
wind, airplane, grass,
clapping,

grass clapping,
birds chirping,

blowing trees,

an eagle.

What do you spy with your little eyes?
I see a grasshopper, leaves, train,
                (choo-choo)
Trains

Train whistle
Trains whistle
And a plane!

bird, grasshoppers, trees, river, sky blue, trees,

        (There's a beehive under the sign,
        you want to see it?)

purple leaves, green leaves, yellow leaves,
water, blue berry, yellow flower,
a grasshopper,
more flowers,
a grasshopper,
boat purple, a purple boat?
seeds in milkweed,
grass, trees, lake,

Big

Mountain

Rocks,

I smell fresh air, smells like wind, air,
smells like air wud,
smells like nothing,
or wood,
and flowers, trees, and flowers

I taste hunger,

      (Still hungry for strawberries—do you have any?)

I'm delicious
I want salad with lettuce, tomatoes, cucumbers,
those bread things, and blue berries

      (You want to taste my rock sandwich?)

I touch soft milkweed rough wood,
grasshopper,
I touched a grasshopper

flowers the air, grass, cotton soft, cottony,

      (I'm tying my shoe. Can you help me? Can you teach me?)

…cottony grass, cotton, milkweed.

      (Will you teach me to tie my shoes?)

      (Like this. Make Rabbit Ears, like I taught my children.)

GrassHopper
Grasshopper

Part III: The Walk Back

We followed breadcrumbs into the woods,
we followed grasshoppers into the woods
with our binoculars
we found so many things.

Artwork by Quran Blocker

A Haiku
by NaQuera Roach and Trinity Jones

We're outside today
There are tall trees with bright leaves
Hear the trains come through

Artwork by Jah'Leigha McSween

The Grasshopper who Resides at Greenport Conservation
by Margaret R. Sáraco

The path that leads to water is simple and generous.
Weeds grow, brown stems lean towards the late afternoon sun,
and blossoms float on a gentle breeze.
I am careful not to veer off path.

The group of children I walk with find a grasshopper,
a happy accident, mesmerized by its green body
stare and recount their discovery,
to each other, to me, to the other adults.

They use magnifying glasses and a camera lens
for a better look. Children are closer to the ground
and don't need to bend quite so far.
I wonder if they know these small marvels

could be green, olive, or brown,
have yellow or red markings,
or that a cloud of them can strip a farmer's crop
bare, munching with their mandibles.

The children might not know,
that they taste with their mouths,
smell with their antennae
and have five eyes.

That's right. Five Eyes--Three simple and two
hexagonally shaped, compound eyes.
Do they know a grasshopper's upper hind leg muscles
are enlarged to let them launch and leap?

I dash ahead with some who need to run
then linger with others who tell stories
about grasshoppers or what they had for lunch.
New to speaking, they have much to tell.

We come to a full stop at the gazebo
no cul-de-sac for them, they see beyond
deep into the ground, looking for other insects
while I take in the expansive

Hudson River below,
the one Pete Seeger sang about.
Many of us downriver, closer to the cities
unknowingly and knowingly polluted, pollute,

and ignored, warning us as children,
if you fall in the Hudson, you need a tetanus shot.
But from my view of the pristine water
it easily reflects the blue sky on a clear afternoon.

I am as amazed by the river as the children are
about the grasshopper hidden in the thicket,
there if you look. If we hadn't been in the woods today
nature's miracles may not have touched us.

It is time to go, and we make our way back
along the trails to their bus, singing songs,
taking pictures, skipping, launching
and leaping like a grasshopper.

Tucked Away
by Margaret R. Sáraco

Pregnant clouds
hold the sun in an embrace.
The woods appear
beyond a small gravel lot.
I am astounded as it opens
before me, framed by

the distant Catskills.
the daylight
barely illuminating
the Access for All Trail
inviting me to walk
and follow dirt arteries
accompanied by
insects and small animals
who peek from tall grass
as they scatter along
the curvy meadow route.

Bluebirds fly
from their boxes
constructed lovingly
by stewards of this land,
one for them and
one built for cranky tree swallows
I believe (and why not)
they direct my attention,
down the trail
(as if the woods were not enough)
to a spectacular view
of the Hudson River below

There, a gazebo, no two,
tucked, wait for me
to sit and think about This Land.

I experience great delight
that comes from discovering
a place, one slip at a time.

Artwork by Alyce Kelly

One Mother Earth
by Margaret R. Sáraco

I am humbled and know my place in the world
when I enter the woods.
Even if I can see a highway from the trail.
it is distant and quieter than driving on it.

But I am struck with how we have compressed nature
to fit our metropolitan lifestyles
thankful for protected lands.
I walk. Don't talk as much as listen.

Why is it we separate or discuss nature
as something other than what we live in every day?
Strange.
Earth is natural.

To be either *In Nature* or *Not In Nature*
is baffling.
I wish we could see Earth as one entity,
show our mother the respect she deserves.

FEATHER RIVER LAND TRUST

 California

The Feather River Land Trust conserves ecologically and culturally important lands and waters in the Feather River Watershed. From Mount Lassen in the north to Sierra Valley in the southeast, the Feather River Watershed spans 2.3 million acres. Even more biodiverse than Yellowstone or Yosemite national parks, the Feather River Watershed is a nationally recognized hotspot for wildlife conservation. The Feather River Watershed provides clean water for 27 million people downstream —for drinking, agriculture, and power.

-Leonhardt Ranch
-Poet workshop leader: Hayli Nicole
-Poets are members of Erica Perdue's class at Quincy High School
-Photos by Hayli Nicole (unless otherwise specified)

Feather River Land Trust

Feather River Land Trust was founded in 2000 by a visionary group of local volunteers. Now a nationally accredited land trust, we're working with grassroots relationships and strategic partnerships to safeguard the Sierra Nevada's largest source of water and ensure that biodiverse ecosystems remain intact and healthy for our shared future.

We accomplish our mission in three primary ways: conserving publicly important lands and waters; maintaining, restoring and enhancing land health and historic and cultural resources; and nurturing and restoring people's relationship to land through nature-based education, recreation, and stewardship activities.

Together with visionary landowners, we're protecting priority private lands for fresh water, wildlife, working ranches, outdoor classrooms, and community spaces where people from all walks of life can cultivate a love of place.

We work with community partners, local ranchers, and Maidu traditional stewardship practitioners to manage lands so that people, plants, and wildlife can thrive. FRLT owns five preserves in five distinct communities across the upper Feather River Watershed. FRLT manages these lands for water, wildlife, low-impact recreation, agriculture, and outdoor education.

Photo by Feather River Land Trust Staff

Learning Landscapes

Learning Landscapes is FRLT's conservation and education program designed to facilitate the nature-kid connection throughout the school year with access to open space, place-based learning, and hands-on stewardship experiences.

While our local kids live in rural communities, quality time outdoors is not a given. Since 2004 we have been working to remedy "nature deficit disorder" in the Feather River region in partnership with school districts, landowners, teachers, and students.

Learning Landscapes pairs the traditional skills of a land trust—working with landowners to protect land and natural resources—with place-based education in partnership with local teachers, school districts, and communities. It's become a national model for outdoor education and fostering a land stewardship ethic in the next generation.

Learning Landscapes seeks to make it easy for teachers and students to get outside, practice science, field journal, and explore. Each school has access to one or more natural outdoor classrooms with a variety of habitats. Each outdoor classroom has a unique landowner agreement, from ownership by FRLT, to school district property, to ownership by private ranchers, public agencies, or companies.

By conserving lands near public schools where daily outdoor education experiences can occur, we create the opportunity for every schoolchild in the region to forge their own lasting relationship with the ground at their feet. Our hope is that no matter where they eventually settle, children from the Feather River Watershed will have learned how to get to know a place, to love a place, and to take care of a place.

LEARNING LANDSCAPES
Nurturing a child's relationship to land and learning

Leonhardt Ranch

The 46-acre property is centrally located in the town of Quincy and extends outdoor education and recreation options for the community. Located across the road from Quincy Jr/Sr High School and a short walk from Quincy Elementary, the Leonhardt Ranch provides a unique, living classroom for hands-on learning and stewardship experiences for Quincy children of all ages.

The land is in constant use by community members, teachers and their students, and the variety of diverse wildlife native to the area. An elevated levy trail follows Boyle Creek, a tributary to Spanish Creek and is a great example of a dynamic landscape. The preserve has wetlands, cattail ponds, willow stands, and big open fields with nearby forest, supporting a diversity of wildlife and birds. Species commonly spotted on the land are beavers, coyotes, frogs, trout, raptors, Sandhill Cranes, Red-winged Blackbirds, waterfowl, and unique songbirds like Bullock's Oriole and Yellow-breasted Chat.

Some outdoor education activities that take place on the land include field journaling, nature observations, and stewardship opportunities. On the west entrance, a structure called Abby's Barn is home to many student projects, including a sign erected by Quincy High School students. The creek on the preserve allows students to take water samples or view wildlife activity and study them in science classes.

In spring of 2022, FRLT staff along with a SNAP AmeriCorps member mentored a local 12th grader completing a senior project at Leonhardt Ranch, training and practicing the use of game trail cameras for environmental science.

Winter Break
by Addison Gay

I go for a walk
Despite the bitter cold
I need a break
From the stress I hold
School
Sports
Work
The fresh air helps
The sun warms me
I need a release
In nature, I find my peace.

Seasons
by Avalynn McColm

Winter brings sorrow
Winter brings death
The cold air hurts my lungs as I take a deep breath
When it gets warmer
Spring arrives with the snow melt
As I look at the flowers I forget the feelings I once felt
Looking at the town I've known my whole life
Its beauty still sticks just like a knife
When summer comes everyone swims
We stay out on the grass as the light grows dim
Soon Fall will come and the leaves will crunch
The cool nights hit hard just like a punch
Soon you remember how you felt in the Winter
The feelings will stick and feel like a splinter
The geese leave in groups of five
The endless cycle will soon revive
Sometimes I feel like the end is near
But then I feel guilt
Because at least I am here.

Untitled
by L.C.

Nature is beautiful,
A place full of life.
Trees and flowers, carpets of clovers,
Underground roots connecting each other,
Reaching out far and touching the stars,
Everything is nature and nature is what you are.

Life's Breath
by D.N.

A breath, fresh air fills your lungs,
The cold wind brushes against your cheeks,
A worm wriggles along the ground
A bird calls out and hundreds reply,
Could it be a cry of defeat, or of victory?
The grass rises and falls
Somewhere a new animal is born
While elsewhere another dies
And yet it carries on, unflinching, unending.
Like a breath it can feel long and satisfying
Or it can feel short, unfulfilling, and pointless,
A chaotic thing that pulls us along,
We end, yet life carries on.

Winter
by Jennifer Kingston

The cold breeze pricking my skin like pins and needles
The mountains draped with a warm blanket
Sleeping
Animals are hidden away running from the soft touch of gentle
snowflakes
Rolling clouds covering the sky in a grey fog
Landscapes and leafless trees glisten with the white icing of snow
Yet birds sing and cars roar on the road not far from me
Nature is frozen under the change in seasons
But life moves on
Changes flicker in my eyes and time moves on ticking
I never liked change
But I learned to appreciate the beauty of the seasons racing by
I think the only reason I can let them past
Is the knowledge that it's not forever
And they're not really meant to last

Nature is Beautiful
by Brianna LaRoche

Owls hooting in the cold nights
Wind flowing through the trees.
The mountains tall and strong just
Like the ocean's high tide.
The soft breeze is like laying in
 a flower field on a cool summer day.
The history of the town gives it a rustic feel
Each forest gives a different sense of comfort
These forests always teaches you something new
There is always something to learn from the forest
and their unique trails and history.

Forgotten.
by L.L.

Nature is dead here.

Everything concrete, as if the life'd never existed

Trees made into houses, sand turned glass-clear.

The people, the cars move on as if they'd never missed it, but—

Out, the city breathes, and with each breath it comes alive

Grass lining the roads, soft leaves under the feet of passerby, shining
feathers on their necklaces and snowflakes suspended from their ears.

Red and orange and green, a streetlight shines down on a mural of a great
oak, encompassing a wall that feels like it came from the dawn of time just
to end up here.

Out, the city breathes, and with each breath it seems like it must die, but

Forever through these streets, nature breathes like it was never to be erased
but rather tempered, made a permanent part of the city's heart—
unforgotten.

I'd Say
by Evelyn Valdivia

Fire. Droughts. Floods.
Rain. Snow. And the beaming hot sun.
Can you see it? Can you feel it?
Summer is finished but it never commenced
Smoke fills the air
Is this our consequence?
Snow flowing into spring
Making the birds silence.
Not once do they sing,
We need guidance.
But the beauty.
Fire brings life
Snow brings memories of snow fights
Rain brings dances
You look up and glance
And you think
"How can a small town, bring so much."
And I'd say
Fire. Droughts. Floods
Rain. Snow. And the beaning hot sun,
Beauty comes from what once was.

Mountains
by Josiah Hardee

Mountains
The spines of the earth
Encasing the lands
Giving the fields depth
Even when under snow
They paint the landscape in beauty,
Making the water flow
Allowing life throughout
Mountains
The depth of the Earth,

Home
by Kaitlynn M.

Cold Autumn Wind
The sun on my skin
Twittering birds, looking for mates
Million pieces of grass, unique, but looking the same
Hundred thousand ants, looking for their queen
Trees on the mountains, mostly evergreens
Water skippers on rushing rivers, trying to survive
It feels like everything in this valley is alive
I am by myself here, but I am not alone
Here, among nature, it feels like I am Home

Quincy
by Lillian Pingree

In the mountains, the air is crisp and clean,
The scenery is breathtaking, like nothing you've seen.
The trees stand tall, and the rivers flow,
In this peaceful place, time seems slow.

Life in the mountains is simple and pure,
The beauty of nature is the ultimate cure.
The wildlife is abundant, from elk to bear,
In this place, you're reminded that life is rare.

The mountains are a place of peace and serenity,
Where the world seems to fade away, and everything is free.
So if you're looking for a place to call home,
Quincy is where your heart will roam.

The City of Hills
by Shelby Nussle

It can't compare to the height of a *skyscraper*
Or the *Color of paint*, painted onto paper
The Millions of Miles they stretch
Simply, you could not *contain* it in a sketch
Oh how they sit still and *unmoved*
Animals and life before it groove
How little a Human is in compare
How Unaware
That a mountain is there in a gaze
Having its ways
Unseen but it stays
Through the days, People stopped and wondered
What a story of a hill holds?
That can't be told.
But an unforeseen sight that will never grow old

The Beauty of Wonder
by Stella White

The wind whispers secrets through the trees
As the sun sets behind the distant hills
A river flows gently in the breeze
And the world is quiet and still

The birds sing sweetly in the morning light
And the flowers bloom in the warm spring air
Nature is a wonder, a glorious sight
A place of beauty beyond compare.

Flower
by T.M.

Flower
Swaying in the breeze
Reaching for the sun
Soft petals of colors
Given as a gift
Tied together with others inside a vase
Liked
Nurtured in a pot
Planted in the soil
Visited by other creatures
Useful for my pollen
Wide eyes staring
Small hands stroking
Loved

Blink
by Z.M.

Blink
Open your eyes.
The forest holds you in its soft embrace
You are safe in the trees where the birds
sing and race
As the deer look on with their surprised face
You are calm.
Blink.
The distant drone of civilization hits your ears
The deer startle and run away as the birds hush and disappear.
You are alone but they are coming.
You hear the saws arrive and
your forest falls to its knees.
Then come the excavators that eat up your beautiful hillside.
You are shocked.
Blink.
The shout of angry men
The drilling and the yelling and the
death of your home.
The animals hit by trucks as survivors are forced into the rapidly dimin-
ishing green.
Your fresh air is tarnished with the smoke and exhaust
You can't move.
You are stuck.
Blink.
You're standing on the cruddy street, suffocated by the identical buildings
and
the screech and honk of traffic.
The children scream and play, surrounded by parents worn to their last
thread
You are intrigued.
How long until the children carry their parents' blank and harrowed
faces?
How long until they're coughing up blood from the black smog that sur-
rounds them?

When will they become just another person
waiting
for their dreams to come find them?
How will they escape the endless cycle.
You are overwhelmed.
Blink.
For a moment,
you are scared.
Scared to open your eyes and see the gray death
But
a cool breeze tickles your face and
beautiful fresh air fills your lungs and
you can finally
breathe.
The branches softly rustle and the birds return
You are surrounded by raw, incredible life.
In the shadows cast by the majestic trees,
you lean back and close your eyes because
here, you are truly free.

JACKSON HOLE LAND TRUST

Wyoming

"Munger Mountain Elementary's 3rd graders embody their mission of biliteracy, bilingualism, academic excellence, equity, and empathy. Their heartfelt poems, a harmonious blend of Spanish and English, capture their experiences at Jackson Hole Land Trust's R Park. Through their words, they showcase the power of connection, embracing nature's beauty to cultivate compassionate hearts and captivating poetry. These young poets are radiant beacons, illuminating the transformative potential of education, empathy, and cultural diversity."

—Bille Metzger, M.A. Ed
3rd Grade Dual Immersion
Munger Mountain Elementary School
Teton County School District #1

-R Park
-Poet workshop leader: Susan Marsh
-Poets are students of Bille Metzger at Munger Mountain Elementary
 School, 3rd grade
-All photos by Zach Andres

Nature es Hermosa
by Vivienne Khusainov, Iris Gutwein, Anonymous-M, Tanner, Thiago
Ayala, Anonymous-A, Anonymous-G, Axel, Alexander B.P., Cristopher
Geovany- Parada-Toledo, Milla Guerrero, Jorge Angel Perez Hernandez

The Water is a milky blue

R- Park es perfecto como tu

El sol resplandece alto en el cielo

The water in the lakes moves really slow

The grass is green so green it should be, it makes me feel free

You find a bay, you go and play

Juego con mis amigos a ser rey

Los Árboles se mecen en el viento suave

Their branches waving passersby

This spring, I sometimes step on crunchy snow, lodo u hijos secas

¡La Naturaleza es nuestra casa!

Poets getting oriented at R Park

El Lugar de la Paz/ Wonderful Moments of R Park
by Marco Muñoz Hernandez, Antonio, August Toal, Dekai Douville,
Finlay Kerr, Alexis Arostico M., CHJ, Yessenia Hernadez, M.J.H., Baylin
Leoni, Dominic Corona

The mountains are big, the world is huge

The reflection of the water over the hills with a calming view

Los pájaros cantado sobre el cielo con el brillosa vista de montaña

Black spiders and centipedes hovering over the water

Los perros corriendo y jugando

Sunshine shining , birds diving with the smell of nature in R Park

The skunk is stinky while we are not

Sun Shining and calling over the R- Park Lake

Con paz en el aire

Winter is coming to an end and Summer is blooming

The water is calm and so are you

El agua esta calma tal usted también

Mountain View by Susan Marsh

El Parque de la Vida
by Haven Ricks, Ana Daniela Alvarado , Gael, Yaretzi Montiel

When I'm at R park I am Joyful

Hay muchas cosas que explorar

R Park is life

R Park is nice

R Park is releasing

Mama Mimi makes me happy

Mama Mimi makes me adventurous

Mi corazón se derrite cuando veo la naturaleza

El agua es calmada y relente

R Park is worth Savoring

Interactive Art at R Park

R Park es Nuestro Parque
by Allison, Ashley Cabrera Garcia, Giselle Perez De Jesus, Tal Filz, Lilian, Anthony Swentosky, LJC, Caroline Heller, Maya Hernandez Kennedy, JG

Rocks on water, trees on land, this is where it all began

El agua es frio y aire esta caliente el viento soplando y las palmas están cayendo

R Park is a sign of life the piece of water, the piece of land sometimes I can feel the sand

Ariba de las montañas, airaba de las colinas, tú puedes encontrar mi aquí

Blazing hot sun or freezing cold snow R Park is the place to go

Ahora podemos hacer R Park nuestro parque

Muy calmado para que todos pueden venir

The sound of water, wind and animal is the sound of life

Ahora tiempo pasa rápidamente y ahora tuvo que irme

Pero si tú quieres encontrarme venga aquí

Winter at R Park

Victorious Poets at R Park

R Park has Amazing Nature
by Nell N., Jessica, Shane Neiswanger, Fernando R.C., Brandon
Hernañdez, Fergus Francis Hannon

Maps shining in the light

This nature is part of my life

El lago está halla cuando miras

La vida es hermosa

Kids play on the shore and the tower of the hill

My life is great but this makes it better

Life is shinning bright

Everything is beautiful even in the night

R Park Arboles
by Lendy, Everett, Bailey M., Yamilet, I.S.S., Max, J.M., Lizeth Loaeza
Luna

Big Mountains in the distance

Crunching sheets of ice and snow

Animales, plantas y personas

Giant Troll, bird songs

Flying ducks and wandering moose

Sparkles in the lake

This place is for everyone

R Park Wildlife

R Park Maravilloso
by Maestra Fio, Soren Berge, Cora McDermott, Fletcher Cozzens, Eddi, Jacob Rojas, Nathan Garcia Garcia, Juan Saldaña, Lyla López, Jade Petrick

Este lugar me hace sentir libertad y calma

Cuando vengo a R Park me siento en paz

Mama Mimi me da tranquilidad como mi mama

R Park es el mejor parque porque no hay basura

Y acoge a los animales

R Park protege la naturaleza

Los peces brincando de alegría

El agua azul calmada

Azul, azul cielo azul

El sol como un abrazo

Poets Contemplate Nature at R Park

The Great R
by Maestra Fio, Soren Berge, Cora McDermott, Fletcher Cozzens, Eddi, Jacob Rojas, Nathan Garcia Garcia, Juan Saldaña, Lyla López, Jade Petrick

Cold and Crispy air

The wood soft and ready to bloom with sticks

Structures like faces and kids

Mama Mimi looks at me like candy

Hills, trees and Mama Mimi Toes

Snow Capped mountains

Water Glowing

Goose and birds singing

Friends and Fresh air

The wind blows

The sunlight

The new grass

The tree that has fallen

The snow beneath my feet

R Park Poets at Work

KENNEBEC LAND TRUST

Maine

The Kennebec Land Trust (KLT) works cooperatively with landowners and communities to conserve the forests, lakes, streams, wetlands, fields, and wildlife that help define central Maine. KLT protects and stewards land permanently, offers access to conserved properties, provides opportunities for people to learn about and enjoy the natural world, and works with partners to support sustainable forestry and farming.

Conservation Across Generations

With a landscape defined by the diversity of the Kennebec and Androscoggin River watersheds, KLT conserves lands and waters in a 413,000-acre service area in Central Maine. The trust was founded thirty-five years ago based on an evolving understanding of the long and complex relationships between people and the land, along with a deep respect for the natural world itself.

We offer places for people to walk in the woods, pause at views of distant mountains and nearby lakes, and hear bird songs and streams running alongside shady trails. These experiences are not just for a few individuals in a given time, but for whole communities and many generations.

-Curtis Homestead Conservation Area
-Poet workshop leader: Ellen M. Taylor
-Poets are 4th grade students of Jennifer Groover, Jude Leaver, and Daniel Gay at Leeds Central School
-Photos by Marie Ring (unless otherwise attributed)

Sustainable Forestry Education Program at the Curtis Homestead Conservation Area

Since 2009 more than 1,000 Central Maine students, parents, and teachers have learned about sustainable forestry during KLT's annual educational program at the 360-acre Curtis Homestead Conservation Area in Leeds. Shortly after KLT acquired the property, Leeds logger Nat Bell suggested that harvesting timber on the property would be a great opportunity to educate local students, teachers, and community members about sustainable forestry.

On this annual field trip, students can observe a timber harvest; see a portable sawmill demonstration; learn more about sustainable forestry and how loggers can protect soil, water, and wildlife; participate in hands-on forestry and Maine wildlife activities; and explore careers related to forestry and forest products businesses.

Nat says, "We always ask the kids, 'What do you guys do in the woods?' Some people hunt. Some people hike. Some people ski. Some people cut firewood. Some people play tag. In a properly managed forest, you can do all of those things. You can grow big, high-value trees. You can have great wildlife habitat for hunting or birdwatching. You can have great trails to go skiing, hiking, walking—anything."

The following individuals and organizations generously contributed time and resources for KLT's 2022 forestry program:
- Nat Bell, logger, Leeds
- Julie Davenport and Shane Duigan, Maine Forest Service District Foresters
- Ken Laustsen, retired Maine State Forest Service biometrician
- Harry Weigman, Maine State Game Warden

Photo (opposite): Nat Bell with Leeds Central School 3rd Graders in the Curtis Sustainable Forestry Education Program

Curtis Homestead Conservation Area – Leeds, Maine, 360 Acres

This land was the family homestead of Archie and Harriet Curtis and their children—Rebecca, Joyce, and Ken, the governor of Maine from 1966 to 1974. The Curtis family grew vegetables, hay, and fruit, and even picked blueberries on the bog. They caught brook trout in local streams and harvested timber with workhorses. In 2000 Governor Ken Curtis and his sister, Rebecca Curtis Meredith, donated 360 acres of their family lands in Leeds to KLT.

Long before the Curtis family arrived in this part of Maine, long before there even was a Maine, this region was a prehistoric crossroads for native people who were traveling between the Kennebec and Androscoggin River watersheds. This area was likely used by Native Americans for hunting, fishing, and harvesting of plants. These same resources brought the Curtis family and more recent residents of Leeds to this community.

This KLT property is open year-round for hiking, bird watching, snowshoeing, cross-country skiing, and other low-impact recreational activities. A network of trails features excellent birding, spring wildflowers, fields, mature forests, an extensive wetland known as a fen, and Bog Brook.

Poem
by Annabella Keim

N Nest bird nest.
A Apple trees.
T Trails Hiking trails.
U upside down i see a upside down tree branch.
R rock there was a very big rock. The rock had spiders on it.
E Exciting to see nature

Annabella Keim

Poem
by Avery Potter

Nest are with the birds

And friends can be family

The birds make me calm

Understanding nature is calming

Reading in the spring makes me happy

Everything is exciting in the spring.

Avery Potter

Poem
by Bode Nile

Pine needles on the ground,
Up in the sky is the shining sun,
Distant birds chirping,
Down under your feet bugs are waking,
Leaves are still on the ground,
Eaves on roofs have no snow.

Season before summer,
Popping color,
Rain
Insects are waking,
Nestled in the tree is a birds nest,
Green grass.

Poem
by C. Piotrowski

Water turns to ice.

Icicles hang from trees.

Night gets longer

The ground is white

Enter the snow enters the earth

Rain turns to snow

Curtis Homestead Conservation Area by Zach Harder

Poem
by GC

No place like the woods
A Lot of trees leaves and mud
Two squirrels share two walnuts
Up on the logs there is a beautiful
waterfall Run to the lake where
the water flows Everyone wants
to go to the creek

Ellen M. Taylor with GC and Noah Rocheville

Poem
by Landon Cote, Leeds, Maine [:

Needles On The Ground Crunch When You Step

Apple Trees Drop Apples For Us

The Branches Fall Off The Trees

Up High Is Were The Top Of The Tree

Ruff Bark Is Hard

Elephants Walk Around Nature

Poem
by Matthew Dunham

N   ight is cold.

A   nts need food.

T   rees need rain and water.

U   mbrellas can keep me dry.

R   oots can be cool.

E   xploring the woods.

Nature calms me,by *Ryker* <3

Nature calms me,the sounds of nature are relaxing, the birds,wind,and trees are all relaxing!The looks of nature are also cool!

Ellen Taylor and Ryker Hillard

Shell
by Kensley Mates

The snail who
    Once lived in the shell has
Moved to a bigger shell
    Once lived on the beach
But now lays in my hand
    So many different shells
But my shell looks like an ice cream cone
    With a hole on the side

Kensley Mates and Abigail Martin

Spring
by Royal Stevens III

The snow is melting
Grass is coming
The sun is hot
Bugs are coming back
A bush is green
The ground is soggy
There are green pine needles
There are red things on the tree
Sun is hot
It makes sweat

Royal Stevens III and Jennifer Groover

The Lonely Branch
by Aubrey Sabine

The lonely branch
sitting all alone
nowhere to go.
Lonely branch
stuck on the grass
and nowhere to go
Now light and delicate
all because it fell
off the heavy tree
Little branch
stuck for ages
Cold and bumpy
from the bark
Be safe and sound
in the ground

Photo: Curtis Homestead
Conservation Area by
Norm Rodrigue

Writing with 4th Graders in Leeds, Maine

by Ellen M. Taylor

—March 27, 2023

They flutter off the school bus like fall
leaves in orange, yellow, and red ski parkas
and snow pants, though this is a spring field trip.
We are writing about nature. Some spread their arms
like birds, some lie like angels on the carpet of snow,
while others skip like stones – all happy to be outside,
away from desks, chairs, fluorescent lights and warning
bells. Here, we sit on fallen trees or leaves. We practice
noticing: chickadees 'song, apple tree buds, dried weeds,
a tiny spider traversing his glacier of snow, jeweled in March
light like a kaleidoscope, like a miracle.

Spring is here; the earth is awakening from winter.
Our surge of sky is bright, bluer than a robin's egg,
bluer than the ocean. What is bark? A tree's best friend,
its skin, protection, maybe? Like a coat? How do you spell
stick? Some twigs have been torn from branches
during recent storms, others decompose, last year's
debris turning to humus, a natural cycle of life
to death. We practice noticing: the breeze, soft,
friendly! the smell of grass – green tufts thrusting
though winter's brittle stubs. Can you eat hay? We are
writing in nature. We are nature, writing. We are

hundreds of miles away from Nashville, where three
4th graders lie dead, pieced with bullets beside their desks.
We know it could happen anywhere, but here we sheltered
by pine and poplar, we are practicing our letters, our powers
of observation, we are writing field notes, we are writing our lives.

SIERRA COUNTY LAND TRUST

SIERRA COUNTY LAND TRUST

California

The Sierra County Land Trust was formed in 2005 to protect open space in the Sierra Buttes/ Lakes Basin and throughout western Sierra County. Our county is blessed with all of the dramatic natural features that the world knows as California's High Sierra.

While much of the Lakes Basin and Sierra County is federally owned in the Tahoe National Forest, there are still many special locations threatened by inappropriate development which could destroy the area's unparalleled scenic, natural, and recreational value. Since our formation, we have preserved over 1600 acres in the Sierra Buttes/Lakes Basin including 2 lakes, much of the saddle that leads hikers to the top of the Buttes, and a large portion of the spectacular face of the Sierra Buttes.

Our goal has expanded to protect important natural lands in all of western Sierra County made up of the important watersheds of the North Yuba River and the Middle Fork of the Yuba River. We take action in the most direct way: by purchasing land and conservation easements and managing these lands to preserve for public use!

-Poet workshop leader: Iain Watson
-Poets are members of Laurie Petterson's class, Loyalton School, Loyalton, CA
-Photos by Stephen M. Carlton

Land Trust Properties for Environmental Experiences

The most popular Land Trust properties where visitors including school children visit include:

Sardine Lake and Upper Sardine Lake

These high elevation lakes offer the most dramatic views of the Sierra Buttes with easy access. Inspiring views of the dramatic Sierra Buttes offer an inspiring "A-Ha!" moment, often life changing experiences for young people. Lessons to be learned include the importance of these high elevation lakes to the water supply of California as well as the importance of protecting forested lands for water quality, wildlife, and climate change mitigation.

The Lookout Tower

Now this is awe inspiring! Students can take the hike on Land Trust property to the old Forest Service Lookout Tower and get a topo map view of the chain of 3 lakes below and a large portion of the Lakes Basin and mountains beyond.

Volcano Lake

An easy hike or ride with our Rangers in ATVs up to a lovely, secluded small mountain lake for a back country experience. Past mining activity can be seen for a discussion of these issues.

Our Youth Program

The Sierra County Land Trust Environmental Education Program is just
forming.

We have been working to support the Downieville School's
environmental education program. The Downieville School is the
small, rural K-12 school that serves much of the high elevation portion
of western Sierra County. They are utilizing the Learning Landscapes
program. To support that program we have located a site on the North
Yuba River for use as an Outdoor School. It is under design now and the
Land Trust will raise funds and volunteers for construction.

Over the long term we are working to create an environmental education
and interpretive program including guided hikes and programs for
visitors and school children on our properties.

Above: The Boathouse at Sunset
Opposite: Above Young America Lake and the two Sardine Lakes

Fall in the Sierra Valley
by Heidi Rahe

In the beginning of fall,
On a cloudless day,
With that light autumn breeze,
It made the trees sway.

Throughout the year,
It had been hot,
But now it's fall,
That cool free thought.

It's taken so long to reach this point,
Through all the days that passed by that I've tallied,
Now that summer has come to a close,
Fall is welcomed to the Sierra Valley.

Above: Mariposa Lily
Opposite: Long Lake and Mt. Elwell

LAND AND WATER

by Cosmo Carr

The land like water flowing in the wind,

The rolling hills like waves of the sea,

The great peaks like tsunamis and hurricanes blazing in the ocean,

Fires burn the mountain yet the rivers flows on,

And yet nature is born anue,

The gold veins of the mountain in the cazum's flow like rivers,

Yet they hide in the streams glinting in the sun,

Hidden by the rocks,

So take this as a reminder to be like the land and water.

SEEING NATURE
by Logan D.

In the time
The outside is quite fine

With the greens & yellows
They keep me quite mellow

Birds chirping, bugs buzzing.
It sounds like discussing.

The earthy smells, wet soil,
it's one thing I will never spoil.

The course wood,
soft and dry plants
Give me a chance

To really see nature.

Above: Shooting Star
Opposite: Ridgeline above Sierra City

THE LEAF THAT LOVED TO LEAP
by Mason Holland

I would love to be a leaf
When I am ready I will leap

In the air I flow like a bird I soar so high
 I might touch the sky

When the cold comes I shiver
After that I might become a small sliver

The snow will cover me in all its might
So I might parish in day or night

Let me be covered so I can fly
If i don't survive, I will be fine

I would love to be a leaf
Remember me as the one that loved to leap

The Elements of Nature

by Calie Jordan

The chilling breeze settled down
The birds chirping made a valiant sound

The sun is shining the warming light
How awesome is the fall breeze when she
Starts her flight

The mountains stand tall at the sight of
The sun shining it very bright light
Making the creek shimmer with all its might

The hawk soars high above
and perches while grabbing a grub
the hawk peers
With his eyes as sharp as a needle
He starts to dive

The mouse gives a squeak at the sight
Of a diving hawk, it's been quite the night

As the day comes to a stop a teardrop falls
From end to end
Good night nature
till daylight comes once again

Opposite: Upper Sardine Lake Reflection

NATURE'S BEAUTY
by Lily Richards

I went to the valley to see what was happening

I felt the wet grass on the cold hard ground

I smelt the wet damp wood in the moist air

The sound of the birds chirping was sweet

Meanwhile I heard the crunching leaves

I saw the fields and the trees surrounding me

When I looked up I saw the bright light cloudless sky

That's all in the beauty of the nature

FALL AND WINTER
by L.M.

Early fall is today,
winter's well on its way

The trees are turning orange, yellow and red

putting colors in my head
All the creatures big and small
are getting ready for the chilly fall

Leaves fall from autumn trees
with a little help from a windy breeze

Harvest is just around the bend
pick the crops thick and thin

Frost on the ground, ice in the wind
winter is coming around the bend

The ground is colder, hard and rough
it's getting cold not cold enough

The one first snowflake--a magical sight

watch as the snow begins to take flight
Fall is over, winter is here
the white snowy ground begins to clear

The bright sun shines on an ocean of snow
the icy ground begins to glow

HOME

By Natella M.

the sky is painted blue,
the ground is stroked with green,
With such a lot of nice fresh air
All splattered together to create
The beautiful place we call home.

Columnar Joints Near Salmon Lake

THERE IS ALWAYS BEAUTY IN NATURE
by J.A.

Like a flower people will grow
bringing a new hope
and a new light for this world
like the sun
they will shine and although
rain will fall like the tears of one
who lost people that they love
even those little glimmering lights
of sadness have beauty in them
and every drop that falls
will help the land to flourish
bringing a new sprout for every one
that Is cut down.

The Wild
by Nevaeh Barney

Sierra Valley, the trees, the air, the pond, the child,
it's all in the wild

You can see the actual animals, scattered around in the pasture
It's all in the wild.

You can see the bitter cold breeze move through the air, I swear.
It's all in the wild.

You can see the cloudless sky not move at all
It's all in the wild.

You can feel the textured leaf and the long wet grass tickle your
leg
It's all in the wild.

You can see the dirty pond not moving at all and the old cricket ridge
bridge
It's all in the wild

Above: Snow Flower
Opposite: View of Sierra Buttes from above Salmon Lake

THE ORANGE AND YELLOW LEAVES
by Stephanie

I see the orange and yellow leaves falling
people are walking
hearing the sound of the crunching
below their feet.
I pick one up,
It's the color of an apricot and lemon
It's ruff and fluffy just like a cloud.
I taste the leaves like fresh mint,
what do you think?
I smell the leaves like old oak.
How fresh it is that it's really great.
Where are the leaves?
They live in the Sierra Valley
in the fall season.

Dragon Tree on Sierra Buttes Trail

CHILDREN OF THE VALLEY
By Iain Watson

Passing beneath
the railroad tracks
the surrounding hills subside,
the flats of faint blonde grass
neighbor the green pastures
dry, thirsty and quiet.

Whispering remnants of
the recent inferno
circulate on the mountainside.

Trees kissed by copper and cardinal
will soon enough undress
and welcome Capricorn.

The crisp and chill air has
chased away the final dog days
while the cows uncaged and content
dot the Sierra Valley.

I wonder what stories lie
between the barb wire and barns-

this city boy will never
comprehend rural life
but will welcome
the calm
the complacent
the simplicity.

To the children of the valley-
continue to care
and cultivate this land
    never forgetting to look up
    to the stars,

for they shine
brighter for you
than they do for me.

Rocks and Sky off of Sierra Buttes Trail

SOLANO LAND TRUST

California

We at Solano Land Trust believe that land is a place of inclusion and solace, benefiting all people— it's a place for community. Our vision is for a land where people can have meaningful outdoor experiences.

-Patwino Worrtla Kodoi Dihi Open Space Park
-Poet and poet workshop leader: Suzanne Bruce
-Participating youth poets are members of Joshua Davis' STEAM class at Golden Hills Community School, 8th grade – 12th grade
-Photos by Solano Land Trust staff

Solano Land Trust

Solano Land Trust was founded in 1986 as the Solano County Farmlands and Open Space Foundation as a result of open space advocates, land developers, and a municipal government working together to benefit the whole community. This unusual genesis created the structure for a board of directors that reflects all sides of land-use issues, united in the mission to preserve the agricultural legacy and natural landscapes of Solano County and enhance people's relationship to the land.

The mission of Solano Land Trust is to inspire a love of the land, and preserve it for people, food, and the natural environment. Our values are focused on land, community, and organizational integrity. While land is at our core, we are not reducible to land. We cannot meet our forever promise without intentional and sustained attention to the community and the organizational integrity necessary to carry our mission forward.

The work we do goes beyond conserving land; it's also about ensuring that people's relationship to the land remains strong. We are committed to building a conservation and stewardship ethic in our community by supporting values based on common ground and engaging the future leaders and land stewards who will come after us to take care of this land.

Through extensive years of outreach and community support, we've been able to offer in-depth studies and programs, expert guidance, and educational tours from our volunteer guides on over 5,000 acres of protected property in Solano County. These K-12 outdoor programs allow students to visit various natural parks and open spaces. We believe that access to natural areas has proven health benefits, from physical health to reduced anxiety and depression. The overall goal is to provide meaningful outdoor experiences to enhance our community's quality of life, health, and social well-being.

At Rush Ranch, they'll experience the rush of exploring acres of historical wetlands, observing native plants and wildlife, and learning about the cultural history of the Patwin Native Americans. At Lynch Canyon, with habitats ranging from steep grasslands to the riparian corridor of Lynch Creek, the property is home to a wide variety of flora and fauna for students to observe. At Jepson Prairie Preserve, students develop an understanding of different habitats and study distinctive plants and animals that reside in the very rare vernal pools. Finally, at Patwino Worrtla Kodoi Dihi Open Space Park, students can learn about the beautiful and cherished blue and live oaks of Solano County.

Solano Land Trust is committed to building new partnerships and strengthening community relationships to ensure that the benefits of land are realized and enjoyed by everyone in our community.

List of Solano Land Trust public properties:
Rush Ranch Open Space - Suisun City, CA
Lynch Canyon Open Space - Fairfield, CA
Patwino Worrtla Kodoi Dihi Open Space Park - Fairfield, CA
Jepson Prairie Preserve - Dixon, CA

Patwino Worrtla Kodoi Dihi Open Space Park

Patwino Worrtla Kodoi Dihi Open Space Park, formerly Rockville Trails Preserve, epitomizes the beauty, rural character, and quiet splendor that is Solano County. Filled with stands of blue and live oaks, temporal vernal pools, wildflowers, and wildlife, Patwino Worrtla Kodoi Dihi's 1,500 acres provide a connection to our past and a vision for our future. As you explore this land, it is easy to imagine a time when Patwin Native Americans walked the oak forests and stood on the highest mesa to look out over the valleys below. The forests, rugged hills and high ridges that they saw hundreds of years ago are largely unchanged.

A vision for Patwino Worrtla Kodoi Dihi Open Space Park is to be a destination where school kids learn about blue oak woodlands, geology, and the land's significance for the native Patwin people for whom it is named. On its paths, people on bikes, on foot, in chairs, and on horses can explore and experience the outdoor beauty of Solano County.

Solano Land Trust will preserve and protect Patwino Worrtla Kodoi Dihi Open Space Park and its biological and cultural resources for generations to come. We value sustaining agriculture on this property and foresee compatible public access, education, and scientific discovery as a means to connect this land with our community.

The All People's Trail

The All People's Trail is a path that is composed of Park Tread. This ADA-approved permeable surfacing material, a proprietary creation of Barth Campbell, is sourced from virgin quarry excavations in eastern Sonoma County and uses a plant-based binding agent. The hills that the trail follows are fairly gentle, but Park Tread can handle a steeper grade than asphalt, as a job at the Zen Center in California's Muir Woods required.

"All other surfaces crack or contract in summer or winter," says Barth. His material passed the snow test in Yosemite National Park. Even sheeting rains will not wash it out.

Like the wideness of the path, the consistent surfacing makes a great difference for wheelchairs, unsteady gaits, and people with limited vision. In order to offer visitors an ideal experience, the All People's Path will be closed to bicyclists and horses, who will use marked bypass trails. The path will also feature an array of 12 by 8 palapa-style shade structures and picnic tables with ride-up access for wheelchairs. And while the park can feel worlds away from the bustle of the Bay Area, the path will connect easily to trails that run through the park and beyond it into the Ridge Trail's Expansive loop system.

Continuing plans for opening Patwino Worrtla Kodoi Dihi Open Space Park to the public

Solano Land Trust is working with First 5 Solano and the Solano Early Learning Consortium to develop a self-guided mindfulness walk through our .25 acre native plant garden and ADA picnic area. The signs will support early childhood educators and service providers, as well as families with young children, by providing a self-guided, trauma informed walk to build resilience through connecting with nature, the present moment and themselves. The signs were developed in partnership and with input by early childhood educators and service providers, specifically for children ages 0-5 and their families.

Connection with Nature—A Cento
by Suzanne Bruce— Inspired by Golden Hills Students

As light shines through every crack
as the birds sing
and the branches of the trees dance,
the world around me so peaceful.

I see the sky,
I feel the wind,
and I can't deny it makes me feel nice,
the wind on my face,
so satisfying.

The delight of nature grows
as I take a sniff of clean, fresh air,
stand aside a rock and stare---

life is like budding flowers,
it can grow into beautiful things,
as I walk through green grass
I look left   and then right,
ask if this amazing day will last.

Night feels so bright,
I look out of my window and see the stars.

Love is a feeling--- not just for a person
but something more,
it is an enjoyment,
feels so nice.

I wouldn't change that for the world.

N.B. This Cento poem is comprised entirely of lines from Golden Hills Community School 8th grade – 12th grade students, Joshua Davis' STEAM class:

(poets' lines in order of appearance)

1, 2, 3: Carlos Gomez-Thurber
4: N.S.
5, 6, 7: SSanna E.
8, 9: MJS. JR.
10, 11, 12: Carlos Gomez-Thurber
13, 14: Kaliyah
15, 16, 17: Carlos Gomez-Thurber
18: Damian C. Aldaco
19: N.S.
20, 21, 22: Kaliyah
23: Damian C. Aldaco
24: N.S.

Interviewing Fairfield, CA Poet Laureate Suzanne Bruce

For people who write poems and other creative works, what might joining a guided hike through nature do to help their practice?

SB: Each time you go and visit a place you're going to see something new and different. You're going to smell different things. You're going to see different textures. You're going to hear different sounds and experience them in a whole different way because they're new. You can write about that experience realistically or you can write about it metaphorically. Each experience is new and exciting even if you've been there 100 times. Open spaces give an opportunity to appreciate the land and its history. I think it's really important to keep land open for creativity, for visual arts as well as writing.

If someone enjoys hiking, birding, and plant identification but hasn't tried their hand at poetry, what can they expect?

SB: I think the first thing they should do if they've never written poetry before is to just journal what they're seeing and what they're experiencing. Jot down words and thoughts and then you can form that into a poem later. I think journaling is important even if you're not a poet. It gives you a chance to write down what you appreciate.

Can you talk about your duties as Fairfield's official Poet Laureate and how that position came about?

SB: I've been writing poetry for many years and there just came a time when I wanted to get other people enthused about writing. Something for people finding their creative voice and for those who already have formed theirs to enhance it. I've been involved in many poetry groups in Benicia, Napa, and St. Helena, and I found that Fairfield was lacking in artistic connections. The city wanted somebody to represent the literary arts and to be an advocate of poetry in the city. As a poet laureate, I am required to write poems for this city, proclamations that I read at City Council meetings, and poetry for downtown celebrations such as the menorah lighting, the Veterans Day parade, and the Fourth of July.

All People's Trail
Patwino Worrtla Kodoi Dihi Open Space Park
by Suzanne Bruce

stepping   where spring has arisen
where carpets of green emblazoned

with white   yellow   red   wildflowers
spreading their robust smiles across vast land

where frisky winds bend blue and live oak tree limbs
coolness streams in between the past and the present

where each step a whisper
and miraculous peace is felt

stepping along All People's Trail
remembering   respecting   recognizing

valued life of Patwins   this trail we share
this timeless view   a kaleidoscope of beauty

in this quiet moment   my mind twirling
vivid awareness   appreciation   gratitude

backside of hills   calmer breezes   I also pause
graceful creek flowing   filled with jovial bounce

water bubbling over tan and grey stones   across the bridge
nemophila baby blue eyes flirt their delicate petals

there are no boundaries here
red tail hawks   spirits of endless sky

fly like musical notes   and I like a symphony
stand in awe   the curve of light on my feet

A place to rest, revel the beauty along the All People's Trail

Tree and human spirits unite as one cannot exist without the other

Workshop Leader-Poet Biographies

Suzanne Bruce holds a B.S. in Education and did graduate work in Behavior Disorders. She taught for over 17 years, and then began writing poetry. Suzanne's poetry is influenced by her years of teaching as well as her experiences as a military wife. Her poems have won several prizes and she has been published in numerous journals. Her books, *Voices Beyond the Canvas* (2007) and *Her Visions Her Voices* (2015), are ekphrastic duets with artist Janet Manalo. She is the current Poet Laureate for Fairfield, CA.

Kara Douglas is a yoga & meditation teacher in Harpswell, Maine. She seeks engagement with nature, where wilderness experiences become a mirror that reflects human complexity and intimacy with our deeper abilities to observe and act. Her work is published in several anthologies including: *Wait, Poems from the Pandemic, A Dangerous New World: Maine Voices on the Climate Crisis* and *From the Mountains to the Sea, The Historic Restoration of the Penobscot River.*

CMarie Fuhrman is a poet, nonfiction writer, educator, and future ancestor. CMarie is Associate Director of the Graduate Program in Creative Writing at Western Colorado University and directs the Elk River Writers Workshop. She lives with dogs and a fish biologist in West Central Idaho where she hikes, camps, and serves as Idaho's Writer in Resident.   CMarieFuhrman.com

Lisa Hibl, PhD is the Director of the Russell Scholars Program at the University of Southern Maine. She teaches a variety of courses with an emphasis on arts and the environment. Her poems have appeared in *Black Fly Review, Hayden's Ferry Review, Hawaii Pacific Review, Untidy Candles: A Maine Poetry Anthology*, and the *Spoon River Anthology*, and she contributed a chapter to *River Voices:Perspectives on the Presumpscot* (North Country Press, 2020).

Susan Marsh lives in Jackson, Wyoming. She has combined her interests in poetry and natural science into a body of work that explores the relationship of humans to the wild. Her poems have appeared in journals including *Deep Wild Journal, Clerestory, Manzanita Review, Parks and Points, Dark Matter, Silver Birch* and others. Her poetry collection is *This Earth Has Been Too Generous* (Finishing Line Press, 2022).

Hayli Nicole is a performance poet and award-winning travel writer. Her years in conservation have inspired her international journeys, including studying orangutans in Sumatra. She believes there is always a story to be found, heard, cherished, and told. Her collection of poetry, *Emergence*, was released in November 2019. Instagram (@haylicans) or read what adventures she's up to next at haylinicole.com.

Margaret R. Sáraco author of the poetry collection *If There Is No Wind* (Human Error Publishing), is a poet, short story writer, former public school math teacher and avid hiker. She has received Honorable Mentions in the Allen Ginsberg Poetry Contest and was nominated for a Pushcart Prize. Margaret enjoys leading writing workshops and helping to create community. Her second collection is due out in 2023. https://linktr.ee/margaretsaraco

Shanley Smith is a poet, storyteller, and budding naturalist. Born in West Michigan, she now calls North Carolina home. Her current work centers around fig trees, cold-nosed dogs, and the benefits of foraging. Shanley's work can be found in *Underground, Mangrove, Collision Literary Magazine*, and *Dimly Lit*. She currently works as the Storyteller & Engagement Liaison at Ox-Bow School of Art and Artists' Residency. You can read more of her writing by subscribing to *Mackerel Skies* on Substack.

Ellen M. Taylor is the author of one chapbook and three collections of poetry: *Humming to Snails, Floating, Compass Rose,* and *Homelands*. Her work has been in the *Café Review, New England Review,* and *North American Review*, among others. She holds a doctorate degree in language, literature, and culture, from Harvard University, and currently teaches literature and writing at the University of Maine at Augusta.

Iain Watson is a 5th generation Nevadan, a third grade teacher, part of the Reno Slam Team, and a founder and director of Spoken Views Collective (SVC), a platform for spoken word poetry and other forms of literary expression. Iain has collaborated with national poetry acts and helped organize a team for the National Poetry Slam and youth teams to Brave New Voices. Iain is a contributor to the Nevada Humanities Heart to Heart series and has been involved in Poetry Out Loud.

About the Editor

Lis McLoughlin holds a BS in Civil Engineering, an MEd in Education, and a PhD in Science and Technology Studies. She founded NatureCulture LLC a green, online media and events company through which she directs the Writing the Land project, and edits and publishes the Writing the Land anthologies, as well as other books. Lis organizes the annual online Authors and Artists Festival. She lives off-grid in Northfield, Massachusetts and part-time in Montréal, Québec. www. nature-culture.net   www.writingtheland.org

About the Foreword Author

Richard Louv is the author of 10 books: *Last Child in the Woods, Our Wild Calling, Vitamin N, The Nature Principle, The Web of Life, Fly Fishing for Sharks, America II, Childhood's Future, 101 Things You Can Do For Our Children's Future,* and *FatherLove.* He co-founded, and is Chairman Emeritus of the Children & Nature Network. Among many other honors, in 2008 he was awarded the Audubon Medal. He is on the editorial board of *Ecopsychology,* and serves on the advisory boards of Biophilic Cities and the International Association of Nature Pedagogy. www.richardlouv.com

About the Project Initiator and Preface Author

Rob Wade is a place-based educator working in the Upper Feather River region of California's northern Sierra Nevada since 1995. He is a founding board member of the Feather River Land Trust, and in 2004 launched Learning Landscapes a K-12 partnership between the Feather River Land Trust, regional schools, and 32 agencies and organizations that support all teachers and over 2000 students annually. In 2017, with support from the Land Trust Alliance, Rob helped establish the national K-12 Community of Practice to support other land trusts to grow enduring and equitable programs for all.

Rob has a BS from the University of California-Berkeley in Conservation & Resource Studies and an MA from the School of Education at the University of San Francisco. Rob is the 2017 recipient of the Excellence in Environmental Education Award, presented by the California Environmental Education Foundation and a 2020 recipient of the Environmental Law Institute's National Wetland Award.

Printed in the USA
CPSIA information can be obtained
at www.ICGtesting.com
JSHW081909191123
52095JS00001B/79